Rest camp in the Kruger National Park

Celebrated for its cast of weird and wonderful creatures, the indigenous wildlife of South Africa is undoubtedly one of the country's most valuable natural assets and tourist attractions. South Africa is a land of diverse and varied landscapes, ranging from the subtropical forests of KwaZulu-Natal to the sun-scorched wilderness of the Karoo, from the Cape Floral Kingdom to the sweeping grasslands of the interior plateau. Each of these unique habitats supports its own distinctive ensemble of plants and animals, creating some of the most biodiverse ecosystems on Earth. While vast herds of game once roamed the length and breadth of the subcontinent, today they exist predominantly in protected conservation areas. Providing a rare glimpse of how humans and nature can prosper side by side, South Africa's vast national parks offer exceptional game viewing throughout the year. The visitor has the opportunity for the ultimate African safari experience: to see the 'Big Five': elephant, rhino, buffalo, leopard and lion.

Preserving a unique natural heritage, precious conservation areas provide a rare glimpse of how Africa used to be.

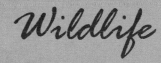

Wildlife

3

White rhino with their distinctively square upper lip

Despite their gentle expressions, buffalo are aggressive

Leopard spend their days lying in seclusion

Welcome to Beautiful South Africa

The southernmost tip of Africa is a land of extreme contrasts. While deceptively green and prosperous in parts, it is barren and desolate in others. In some areas the country is spectacularly mountainous, while elsewhere it is a landscape of endless plains, stretching to the distant horizon. Consistent, however, are South Africa's enduring beauty and the warmth of its people: this is a renowned for its magnificent coastline, rugged mountain profile, undulating deserts and the hospitality offered by its multicultural populace, united in their passion for this land with its wide open skies and endlessly forgiving climate. Coastal cities like Durban, Port Elizabeth and Cape Town are cosmopolitan in flavour, their beaches warm and welcoming, their attractions varied and vibrant. Inland, Johannesburg, Bloemfontein, Pretoria and Nelspruit are the capitals of industry, hubs of the country's economy. South Africa is substantially rich in minerals – gold, platinum, coal and diamonds, and its history records many lively stories of settlers who flocked from afar in search of fame and fortune during the legendary 'gold rush' days. The country enjoys a moderate climate. Its eastern shores are washed by the warm Indian Ocean, and sub-tropical climatic conditions bring hot summers, exceptionally mild winters and summer rainfall. Clear, sunny, yet cool winter days and warm summers are characteristic of the inland Highveld regions. The westerly reaches of the country experience very dry and hot summers, with cold, damp winters, consistent with a Mediterranean climate.

The giraffe is the tallest land animal and can grow to a height of more than five metres

When it comes to seeing wildlife in its natural habitat, few places can compare to the sheer size and diversity of the renowned *Kruger National Park*, one of South Africa's foremost sightseeing destinations. The park covers more than 20 000 square kilometres of the Mpumalanga Lowveld, and its spectacular subtropical bushveld is home to nearly 150 species of mammals, more than 500 birds and over 100 reptiles. Half an hour's drive from Port Elizabeth, *Addo Elephant National Park* was established in 1931 to preserve the 11 elephants that had survived extensive human settlement and hunting in the area. Addo now provides sanctuary to more than 450 graceful pachyderms. Recently the park has been extended over the freeway to the coast, and is now very proud of its uniqueness in having the 'Big Six', which includes the whale. *Hluhluwe Imfolozi Park* is situated on the North Coast of KwaZulu-Natal and is the oldest game reserve in Africa. Proclaimed in 1895, it is renowned for the success of its conservation efforts, most notably for bringing the white rhino species back from the brink of extinction. The rich diversity of vegetation in the park supports a multitude of wildlife, including the 'Big Five'.

Grey crowned cranes inhabit dry savannah

The distinctive stripes of the Burchell's zebra

A herd of elephant cows and their calves make their way across the bushveld

Silhouettes of gemsbok at sunset

Xhosa circumcision initiates in the Eastern Cape

A Zulu warrior in traditional dress

Bushmen hunter-gatherers of the Kalahari Desert

Zulus are the largest ethnic group in South Africa

A veritable melting pot of cultural, ethnic, social, ancestral and religious traditions, South Africa's 'Rainbow Nation' brings together a profusion of African, Asian and European influences. Each of the country's nine provinces offers its own unique history, landscape and character, extending from the European and Malay essence of the Cape to the Xhosa, Zulu, Indian and colonial English influences that have made their mark all along the coast up to the north of KwaZulu-Natal. The vast interior has witnessed its own cultural evolution, with the emergence of the distinctive Afrikaner national identity and the flowering of the Sotho and Tswana cultural traditions. A land of conflict and conciliation, more than 40 million people live in South Africa, with over a third of these now living in the cosmopolitan urban centres of greater Johannesburg, Durban, Cape Town and Port Elizabeth. In recent years, mass urbanisation, the transition to democracy and the increasing influence of globalisation have prompted the emergence of vibrant new cultural identities.

A richly contrasting and unforgettable land of remarkable heritage and cultural history as complex as it is fascinating.

People of South Africa

Resourceful residents have created makeshift homes in the many informal settlements around South Africa

Grand entrance to a world of opulent luxury

Hidden in the Pilanesberg Mountains, close to the town of Rustenburg in the North West Province, is a holiday destination of breath-taking proportions.

The Lost City

The most recent addition to the extensive resort complex Sun City, *The Palace of the Lost City* was the realisation of hotel magnate Sol Kerzner's creative vision to build what resembles an ancient ruined city that has returned to its former glory. Central to the Lost City is the Palace at the Lost City, a hotel built in grand ethnic style with a magnificent courtyard and surrounded by elaborate and exotic gardens, tropical forests and rocky water features. The Palace offers sumptuous luxury at every turn, with rich tapestries and hand-carved furniture, bold bronze statues and intricate mosaics. Opulence echoes from every corner, no luxury is spared and no detail has been overlooked in the extravagant indulgence of guests. Sun City is set on the edge of an immense volcanic crater within the Pilanesberg mountains. One of the largest volcanic formations of its type, this unique habitat forms the nucleus of the *Pilanesberg National Park*. One of the biggest in Southern Africa, the park is highly regarded for its prolific birdlife and rich biodiversity.

A view of The Palace across the Bridge of Time

Mighty Shawu is the centrepiece of the Elephant Atrium

The 338-room luxury hotel is surrounded by a vast botanical jungle landscaped with flowing cascades, pools and featuring the exhilarating Valley of the Waves adventure park

Pretoria is renowned for its jacaranda trees

The principal cities of
Johannesburg and Pretoria make
up Gauteng, the nation's bustling
commercial and
industrial centre.

Gauteng

Johannesburg is often referred to as 'Egoli': the City of Gold. In 1886, gold was discovered on the dusty, desolate plains of the Witwatersrand, and the city mushroomed around the site as word spread of its potential; settlers flocked in search of a lucky find. Today, Johannesburg is the financial capital of South Africa and a thriving metropolis of elaborate office parks and towering buildings, elite residential suburbs and bustling shopping malls, restaurants and entertainment venues.

Established on the outskirts of Johannesburg at the height of apartheid, *Soweto* first came to the world's attention on June 16, 1976, when police opened fire on protesting schoolchildren. These days, guided tours of this vibrant residential area draw thousands of enthusiastic visitors.

Historic *Pretoria*, approximately 40 kilometres from Johannesburg is South Africa's capital and is home to the Union Buildings, the country's administrative centre. It is also the venue for prominent political celebrations – this is where the first President of the newly democratic South Africa, the charismatic and highly respected Nelson Mandela was inaugurated in 1994. Streets lined with exotic jacaranda trees add to the allure of the city, which harmoniously combines the gracefully restored buildings of yesteryear with fine examples of modern architecture.

The Hillbrow Tower dominates the skyline above Johannesburg's built-up inner city

Hector Pieterson Memorial in Soweto

Densely populated Soweto

Nelson Mandela Square in Sandton

God's Window offers a spectacular vista

Misty country roads, acres of dense forest, breathtaking views and quaint villages make Mpumalanga a place of beauty and tranquillity.

Mpumalanga

The climate of the escarpment renders this ideal timber country. Thousands of acres are devoted entirely to forestry, and several towns in the area owe their existence to this industry, including Graskop, which was once a small gold-mining village.

The colourful history of *Pilgrim's Rest* as a mining town is preserved in its corrugated-iron rooftops and Victorian era bungalows. Gold was discovered here in 1873, and the once-peaceful valley became the scene of frenetic digging and frenzied activity as prospectors arrived in their droves in search of fame and fortune. Some left with shattered hopes, others remained, swept along by the feverish rush for gold. The timber-mining town of *Sabie* enchants the visitor with casual charm and sincere hospitality. The roads into and out of the town pass by beautiful waterfalls as numerous rivers wind their way onward to the sea.

Pilgrim's Rest has preserved much of its 19th century charm

Mpumalanga province is blessed with an abundance of forests, rivers and waterfalls including the spectacular Berlin Falls

Up to 700 metres deep and 60 kilometres long, the Blyde River Canyon is the third-largest canyon in the world

Stalactites and stalagmites in the Sudwala Caves

Sunset over the escarpment

Three Rondawels - an icon of the Blyde River Canyon

From *God's Window*, the land falls away from the great escarpment into the vast forested Lowveld, often swathed in mist. In early winter, the view is framed by glowing orange aloes, and visitors can best appreciate this panoramic corner of the world from this site.

The curious quirks of water in motion have left extraordinary potholes in the rocks of the Blyde River. These are known as *Bourke's Luck Potholes*, after the owner of a once-profitable gold mine nearby. A natural marvel up to 700 metres deep, the *Blyde River Canyon* is the third largest canyon in the world and from the dramatic cliffs of the escarpment above, provides some of the most striking scenery in Mpumalanga. The Blyde River (meaning 'River of Joy') was named by the wives of Voortrekkers who, after assuming that their menfolk were dead when they did not return from an expedition, encountered them as they made their way along the banks of the river. The Blyde flows through some spectacular gorges along its course, and meets with the Blyde Dam in its canyon at the nature reserve.

Formed in prehistoric sedimentary rock on the Drakensberg escarpment nearly 250 million years ago, the *Sudwala Caves* are the oldest known caves in the world. The caves consist of a series of vast caverns, where the dramatic rock formations provide a glimpse of Earth's evolution.

Bourke's Luck Potholes

uShaka Marine World

An inviting holiday
playground, with miles of
glorious golden beaches washed
by a warm ocean.

KwaZulu-Natal

including Durban, South Coast and
North Coast

Durban is a leading destination among local holidaymakers, and is blessed with spectacular swimming beaches and a warm climate throughout the year. As one of South Africa's most ethnically diverse cities, Durban bears the hallmarks of Asian, European and African cultural influences. Constructed on the edge of the ocean, uShaka Marine World is one of the city's leading tourist attractions and features an innovative shipwreck-themed aquarium and aquatic amusement park with an architectural style richly influenced by Zulu culture.

Durban's ever popular 'Golden Mile'

Margate's mile-long beach is ideal for swimming

Fishermen with their catch during the sardine run

Suspension bridge over the uMthamvuna River

The *South Coast* extends south of Durban and beyond Port Edward to the Umthamvuna River. The route is dotted with sleepy resort towns set amid a lush subtropical paradise and offers miles of unspoiled golden beaches bounded by warm ocean waters. Margate is the South Coast's most popular holiday town and accommodates more visitors than residents. Holidaymakers are perennially drawn to Margate by its expansive beaches, agreeable climate and laid-back atmosphere. Added attractions to this charming town include fishing, diving, whale-watching, golf and hiking. In the middle of each year, one of the great wonders of the natural world takes place along the South Coast as vast shoals of sardines migrate up the coast from the colder waters off the Eastern Cape. Billed as 'the greatest shoal on earth', the annual sardine run attracts sharks, dolphins and a frenzy of sea birds, all squabbling over this vast, moving feast. Thousands of eager fishermen also join the fray, anxious to catch their share of the ocean's bounty. Inland from Port Shepstone, the Mzimkulwana River has carved a spectacular sandstone canyon known as Oribi Gorge. An important conservation area, the 24-kilometre gorge forms part of the Oribi Gorge Nature Reserve. The reserve offers spectacular views and is sanctuary to an abundance of birdlife and small mammals, including the oribi, the rare grassland antelope after which the gorge is named.

A sightseeing cruise on the St Lucia Estuary

Hluhluwe Imfolozi is Africa's oldest national park

Umhlanga at sunset

The **North Coast** is a vast territory once ruled over by Shaka and his mighty impis and, generally speaking, is less developed than the South Coast. While much of the region was turned over to cultivation, with extensive tree and sugar plantations, vast areas remain untamed. Past the upmarket beach resorts of Umhlanga Rocks and Ballito and beyond the Tugela River lie the unspoiled game reserves of the Greater St Lucia Wetland Park, Mkhuze and the remote wilderness of Maputaland and Kosi Bay. The St Lucia Estuary (Isimangaliso Wetland Park) is a proclaimed World Heritage Site, its rare wetland habitat being a haven for the protection of wildlife, including hippos and crocodiles, and for the preservation of indigenous plant and marine life. On the hills of northern KwaZulu-Natal stand the traditional homes of the once-feared Zulu nation. Tribal custom and ceremony reign supreme here, and in their elaborate beadwork the women weave messages of hope, love and virtue.

Dozens of fishermen cast their lines at Cape Vidal on the pristine shores of the Greater St Lucia Wetland Park

A burst of autumn colours forestall winter's arrival

A vast heritage of ancient valleys and towering peaks, The Drakensberg's history is hidden in the depths of caves and rock shelters

Midlands & Drakensberg

Unspoiled farming country with rolling green hills and a cooler climate than the subtropical coastline, the *KwaZulu-Natal Midlands* has recently become the focal point of a thriving arts industry. The self-guided Midlands Meander route offers visitors the opportunity to drop in on artists at work crafting elegant wrought-iron pieces, earthenware, leather goods, elaborate paintings, furniture, wooden homeware, clothing and much more. Several country inns and hotels en route complete a leisurely excursion through the Midlands, offering warm hospitality and hearty country fare.

Beyond its gentle foothills, *The Drakensberg* – meaning 'mountains of the dragon' in Afrikaans – creates an imposing boundary between KwaZulu-Natal and Lesotho. Crisscrossed by icy streams and swiftly-flowing rivers, blessed with plentiful animal and bird life and rich with history, the Drakensberg is a place where silence echoes among valleys of timeless beauty and peaks reach staggering heights. In recognition of its spectacular scenery and diverse ecology, the mountain region of the uKhahlamba-Drakensberg Park was declared a World Heritage Site in November 2000.

Early morning light falls across this beautiful region of the Drakensberg

The basalt peaks of the Drakensberg are known by the Zulu and Sotho peoples as *uKhahlamba*, meaning 'barrier of spears', and were formed by deposits of volcanic lava more than 120 million years ago. Ancient Bushmen have left priceless evidence of their presence in the Drakensberg centuries ago. Rock art found in the caves and shelters beneath the mountains provides clues to their way of life. In the north lies the spectacular Amphitheatre, a crescent-shaped wall of solid basalt, guarded by the 3 165-metre Sentinel and the 3 009-metre Eastern Buttress. Several rivers have their source high up in these mountains, including the Orange River, which follows a 2 200-kilometre course to the Atlantic. The uThukela River has its origin here too and creates some spectacular waterfalls and exquisitely scenic landscapes on its journey to the sea. Occasionally, seasonal snowfalls transform the dry, brown landscape into a spectacular winter wonderland.

Drakensberg resorts are renowned for their cosy accommodation, wholesome foods and welcoming ambience. Amid the spectacular mountain setting, recreational sports abound, with hiking, horse riding, mountain biking and fishing among the popular pursuits.

The rugged landscape of the 'barrier of spears'

Trout fishing is popular in the Southern Drakensberg

The Amphitheatre provides a majestic backdrop to the tranquil waters of the uThukela River

Sun-kissed sandstone cliffs at Golden Gate

From the vast fields of sunflowers to an endless sea of maize fields, the enormous plateau appears gold in colour.

Free State

Predominantly farmland, this 'Big Sky Province' invites you into a world of quiet remote villages, wide open spaces and vast tracts under cultivation. A massive layer of sandstone which stretches along the Eastern Free State border with Lesotho has been eroded by the elements and, over time, flat-topped rock formations have evolved. A visual highlight of the province, this landscape of sheer cliffs literally glows red, orange and yellow according to the quality of the sunlight. *The Golden Gate Highlands National Park* was proclaimed to conserve almost 5 000 hectares of this remarkable land, while also protecting a multitude of plant and animal species.

South Africa's major waterway, the *Orange River* forms the province's southern border. The 374-square-kilometre Gariep Dam was constructed to harness the power of the river and to provide a stable water source for the Orange River Basin and vast areas of the Eastern Cape.

The provincial capital, *Bloemfontein* – meaning 'flower spring' in Afrikaans – was named after the natural spring waters which quenched the thirsts of the hunters, Voortrekkers, traders and missionaries who crossed these central plains. Monuments and statues throughout the city pay tribute to the forefathers, presidents and statesmen who shaped the history of this landlocked province.

A quiet byway meanders through idyllic countryside

Undulating landscape reaches as far as the eye can see

Cosmos and sunflowers paint vast swathes of vibrant pastel and yellow across the Free State grasslands

Valley of Desolation near Graaff-Reinet

The picturesque Eastern Cape is as rich in history as it is in scenic wonders.

Eastern Cape

The vast Eastern Cape presents a wide variety of landscapes, ranging from desolate sandy beaches, wooded mountains and hilly grasslands to the great arid plains of the Karoo hinterland. A major regional commercial centre, *East London* is South Africa's only major river port and, with its consistently good waves and excellent swimming beaches, a popular seaside resort. The coastline is washed by the warm Indian Ocean, and several resort towns have been established to take advantage of the natural golden beaches that stretch along the coastline.

Port Alfred, on the Kowie River, once a port for vessels that could navigate it's challenging entrance, now offers a haven for pleasure craft, safe swimming beaches and one of the most magnificent golf courses in the country.

Known as the 'friendly city', *Port Elizabeth* combines a fascinating history with a glorious seaside setting. Once on the frontier of the Cape Colony, it was here that the 1820 settlers disembarked in one of the first waves of British immigration to South Africa. The city's attractions range from its settler heritage and historic buildings to an oceanarium and spectacular swimming beaches.

Renowned as the 'City of Saints', *Grahamstown* is steeped in history, its tall church spires recalling the days when the town was a settler stronghold. Today, it distinguishes itself as an education centre and is the home of Rhodes University.

A little oasis nestling between the rocky hills of the Karoo, the old-world town of *Graaff-Reinet* is bordered in the west by the Valley of Desolation, so named because of the gnarled and craggy cliffs, lofty towers of rock and the oddly shaped spires which the elements have fashioned over the ages.

East London boasts South Africa's only major river port and is a popular seaside holiday destination

Port Elizabeth's beachfront

Recreational watercraft moored at the Port Alfred Marina

Grahamstown is rich in Victorian and settler heritage

The Tsitsikamma National Park offers a rich variety of facilities in an idyllic setting, including their spectacularly positioned seaside chalets

The lure of magnificent beaches, an exquisite natural environment and world-class recreational facilities make the Garden Route one of South Africa's most popular tourist destinations.

A compelling highlight of the Garden Route, the *Storms River* surges through a deep gorge into unforgiving ocean swells at the celebrated Tsitsikamma National Park.

Plettenberg Bay is a seaside playground of the well-to-do. This is a little town with a big reputation – its exquisite setting, magnificent beaches and vibrant social scene have confirmed Plettenberg Bay's position as the most fashionable resort on the Garden Route.

Situated on the edge of South Africa's largest indigenous forest and alongside a vast tidal lagoon, *Knysna* has grown from a sleepy backwater into one of South Africa's leading tourist stopovers. Its most famous landmark is the Knysna Heads, a pair of giant sandstone cliffs that dominate the landscape at the mouth of the lagoon.

Nature's Valley is ringed by indigenous forests

Between mountains and ocean lies a magnificent coastline unrivalled for its scenic splendour

The Garden Route

The untamed beauty of Storms River Mouth has made it a destination of choice for many visitors

Set on the edge of South Africa's largest inland salt-water lake, the low-key town of *Sedgefield* has become an increasingly well-known destination for birdwatchers, fishermen and water sports enthusiasts.

An ideal destination for those in search of a relaxing retreat in an exceptional natural environment, *Wilderness* is set amid a system of lakes and estuaries, and blessed with miles of uninterrupted sandy beaches.

Once described as 'The prettiest village on the face of the earth', *George* lies at the foot of the towering Outeniqua Mountains. South Africa's sixth oldest town, it abounds with historical charm and character. A glorious reminder of a bygone era, George's Outeniqua Railway Museum operates the Outeniqua Choo-Tjoe, the last steam-driven scheduled passenger train operating in South Africa, which follows a spectacular route along the coast to Knysna.

The old-world harbour town of *Mossel Bay* is the birthplace of modern South African history. It was here, under the leadership of the Portuguese explorer Bartholomeu Dias, that Europeans first set foot on Southern African soil in 1488. Today, this rich history is celebrated at the Dias Museum Complex, which incorporates fascinating maritime, local history and shell museums as well as the famous Post Office Tree.

A suspension bridge spans Storms River Mouth

Plettenberg Bay's vibrant town centre

Swartvlei is South Africa's largest inland salt-water lake

The Knysna Lagoon spills into the sea at the Heads

Beacon Isle Hotel, Plettenberg Bay

Paul Sauer Bridge spans the Storms River Gorge

An aerial view highlights Knysna's remarkable setting and stupendous natural attractions.

A grand 19th century 'ostrich palace'

The harsh beauty of this arid landscape reveals a region of charming character and contrast.

The Karoo & Cango Caves

The Cape's vast interior is a remarkable semi-desert region falling in the rain shadow created by the Cape fold mountain chain that separates the dry plateau from the lush coastal belt. 'Karoo' is a Khoi word meaning 'hard and dry' and the climate here is made all the more challenging by the extremely hot summers and chilly winters.

To the north of the Swartberg Mountains lies the *The Great Karoo*, an arid hinterland that boasts the largest variety of desert flora in the world, with more than 9 000 species having been recorded.

The Little Karoo is situated between the Outeniqua and the Swartberg Mountains. This fertile region presents a patchwork landscape of irrigated fields and undisturbed fynbos. The climate is not as harsh as upcountry and the vegetation is rich with proteas, watsonias and other wild flowers.

The ostrich capital of the world, *Oudtshoorn* owes its fame and prosperity almost entirely to the world's largest flightless bird and the lucrative industry that has sprung up around it. Before the first World War, ostrich feathers were in great demand by fashion houses in Europe. Today ostrich farms produce leather, biltong, feathers and intriguingly large ostrich eggs.

An important agricultural centre where the climate is well suited to the cultivation of port wine grapes. *Calitzdorp* is the origin of a number of world-renowned dessert wines.

Taking in some of the harshest and most beautiful countryside the southwest Cape has to offer, the meandering byways of *Route 62* boast the Cape's longest wine route.

Ostrich farming near Oudtshoorn

The Cango Caves comprise a vast network of magnificent limestone caverns extending beneath the foothills of the Swartberg Mountains

Breathtaking rock formations adorn the Cango Caves

Formations of folded rock in the Swartberg Mountains

The route leading up the Swartberg Pass

This part of the continent was once below the ocean. Well after the ocean receded, the *Cango Caves* began to form some 20 million years ago as ground water seeped through the limestone, creating cavities and underground tunnels. Rivers on the surface eventually found their way through these cavities, scouring out ever greater tunnels and cavities. Roughly four million years ago, the wonderland of eerie stalagmite, stalactite and other formations began; some dainty and intricate, others hauntingly grotesque.

Part of a system of Cape fold mountains formed millions of years ago, the rugged *Swartberg Mountains* separate the broad valley of the Little Karoo from the Great Karoo that lies to the north. The range is the highest in the Western Cape and includes the province's highest peak, the 2 325-metre Seweweekspoortpiek. The mountain chain is well known for its spectacular mountain passes and impressive views.

The spectacular 23-kilometre *Swartberg Pass* links the Karoo town of *Prince Albert* with the Little Karoo. It was completed by Thomas Bain in 1888 using convict labour. In steep, mountainous countryside this scenic roadway twists and turns through a rugged landscape to a height of 1 585-metres before descending past the Cango Caves to Oudtshoorn.

A scattering of fertile farmland dots the low ground beneath the Swartberg Mountains

Once a sleepy fishing villlage, Hermanus has developed into a busy tourist centre and whale watching destination

Fields of yellow canola in the Caledon district

Lying to the east of the Cape Peninsula, this region yields export-quality fruit and its lush farmlands supply much of the country's wheat and barley. Rich in history, its small country towns with their whitewashed, gabled buildings, 'broekie lace' filigree wrought-iron decoration and good old-fashioned hospitality, recall days of an unhurried rural existence and carry the names of the men who helped shape their early development: *Stanford*, *Swellendam* and *Caledon*. The Overberg boasts some of the finest areas of fynbos in the country, and its largely undeveloped coastline is host to a great variety of aquatic birds and many species of marine life.

Every year visitors flock to the sunny coastal town of *Hermanus*, the heart of the Whale Coast, where they can enjoy the best land-based whale watching in the world. Southern right whales leave the icy Antarctic to calve in warmer waters and as many as one hundred find refuge in Walker Bay between July and December, coming in as close as ten metres from the shore.

A tranquil corner of the Cape Province, where golden wheatfields and acres of fertile valleys meet rocky cliffs and tumble onto sunwashed beaches.

The Overberg

Robben Island

"This Cape is the most stately thing and the fairest Cape we saw in the whole circumference of the earth" - Sir Francis Drake.

Cape Peninsula

The Cape Peninsula combines the finest scenic treasures with infinite character, charm, a proud history and colourful, cosmopolitan people to offer visitors an unrivalled holiday experience. The southeastern slopes of Table Mountain are devoted to the preservation of South Africa's magnificent floral heritage at the Kirstenbosch National Botanical Garden. The beaches along the Peninsula may be described, quite simply, as glorious. Miles of crisp, white sand are washed by the clean, clear waters of the chilly Atlantic Ocean on the west coast, and the warmer Indian Ocean in the east.

Clinging to the sheer slopes beneath Lion's Head, lies some of the most expensive real estate in Africa. Below theses exclusive residences, *Clifton's* four beaches, separated and sheltered by great boulders, are a magnet for the fashionable set who want to see and be seen.

The lawns at popular *Camps Bay* sweep down to a large, sunny beach. The Atlantic coastline is a much sought-after residential area, with grand, multi-storeyed buildings and elegant apartments reaching from the beach right up onto the mountain slopes.

At Cape Town's *V&A Waterfront*, neglected warehouses have been skilfully transformed to create a quaint dockland of museums, taverns, shops and hotels, which integrate the grace of the Victorian era with a distinctly nautical theme.

Enveloped in clouds, the towering slopes of Table Mountain provide a magnificent backdrop to the historical dockside buildings of the Victoria & Alfred Waterfront

Kirstenbosch National Botanical Garden

Cable cars rise to the summit of Table Mountain

The tip of the African continent at Cape Point

The exclusive suburb of Camps Bay stretches out beneath the rocky slopes of the Twelve Apostles

Cape Point is a headland known for its exquisite beauty and countless shipwrecks, here the southern tip of the Cape Peninsula plunges down into the merciless depths of the Atlantic Ocean.

Lying more than ten kilometres offshore is *Robben Island*, the infamous prison island where Nelson Mandela was incarcerated with many of his comrades and now a UNESCO World Heritage Site. Informative tours of the maximum security prison are conducted by former political prisoners.

One of the World's most recognisable landmarks, *Table Mountain* has been created by the erosion of sandstone over the last 450 million years. The panoramic vista from its 1086-metre summit provides a spectacular view of the city below and the distant shores of the magnificent Atlantic coastline. Flanked by the unmistakable mound of Lion's Head rising up in the west and Devil's Peak to the east, on a clear day this unique bastion of rock can be seen from more than 100 kilometres out to sea.

A postcard perfect view of Table Mountain, as seen from Bloubergstrand

Established in 1685, Groot Constantia is one of South Africa's oldest wine estates

Cape governor Simon van der Stel is credited with the first success in cultivating the quality of grapes required for the making of fine wines and in 1685 he was granted the farm *Groot Constantia* in recognition of his services as commander of the Dutch East Indian Company.

Leaving religious persecution behind them, French Huguenots brought their wine-making skills to the Drakenstein Valley in the 1680s. Now one of the most fashionable destinations in the winelands, *Franschhoek* has gained popularity as a centre for wine appreciation and fine dining.

With its oak-lined streets and 17th and 18th century architecture, the historic university town of *Stellenbosch* lies at the heart of the Cape wine routes and is an ideal base from which to explore the hundred or more estates in the region.

Paarl is known as the 'pearl' of the Berg River Valley and produces many of South Africa's most well-loved and award-winning wines and features a number of picturesque old estate homes set in spectacular surroundings.

A classically gabled Cape Dutch homestead

Valley after fertile valley, a colourful patchwork of scenic beauty.

Cape Winelands

Paarl lies in the heart of the Cape winelands

Autumn shades colour vineyards near Stellenbosch

Rugged Atlantic coastline near Saldanha Bay

Many of the natural bays along the Cape West Coast were named after the navigators and discoverers who explored the hazardous coast of this rugged land.

West Coast

A popular family resort situated on the sheltered margins of an exquisite lagoon, the calm waters of *Langebaan* are surrounded by old-world fishing villages and Cape Dutch farmsteads.

West Coast National Park is one of the many highlights of a visit to the West Coast. The park was established to protect the diversity of marine life, flora and fauna in the Langebaan Lagoon and the exceptional coastal wetlands that surround it.

With a water surface larger than the harbours of Cape Town, Port Elizabeth, East London and Durban combined, *Saldanha Bay* is South Africa's largest and deepest natural harbour. It was discovered by Portuguese navigator Antonio de Saldanha in 1503 and is an important fishing centre.

From its early years as a small fishing settlement, *Lambert's Bay* has developed into a busy holiday town. Bird Island is a leading attraction and a cacophonous breeding ground for thousands of jackass penguins, Cape gannets and cormorants.

In a time-honoured tradition, the fishermen of *Velddrif* still cast their nets from colourful little boats here on the tranquil and slow flowing waters of the Berg River estuary.

When adequate rain falls over the dry and desolate *Namaqualand* at the end of winter and the scorching desert winds hold their force, a miracle occurs: from the parched and arid desert land burst forth a wild profusion of blossoms in a sea of vivid colours.

A carpet of bright blossoms stretches as far as the eye can see: a glorious scene during springtime in Namaqualand

Brightly painted West Coast fishing boats

The quiet waters of the Berg River estuary at Velddrif

Langebaan Lagoon is a highlight of the West Coast

Water rushes over the Augrabies Falls

The Northern Cape is the largest
of South Africa's provinces,
spanning from the diamond
encrusted Atlantic shores to the
dry wilderness.

Northern Cape

The vast open spaces of the Northern Cape ensure that the province's many natural and historical attractions lie far apart, its quaint hotels and inns providing welcome refreshment to travel-weary holidaymakers, who have risen to the challenge of visiting these far-off parts. The wilderness is so dry here that in a single year there is less rainfall than some European cities record in a day.

When diamonds were found in the walls of a *Kimberley* farmhouse in 1869, the discovery sparked a world-wide diamond rush of immense proportions. So great was the determination of the diggers to uncover the earth's diamond cache that a small hill was demolished by their efforts, and the 457-metre 'Big Hole' was mined entirely by hand with picks and shovels.

Offering an unforgettable sensory experience, the thundering waters of the Orange River surge down a sheer 56-metre wall of granite to create Africa's second largest waterfall. The *Augrabies Falls* derive their name from the Khoi word meaning 'place of great noise' and, in times of flood, as many as 19 separate waterfalls tumble into the gorge.

The Kalahari grasslands support a host of wildlife

The 'Big Hole' excavation site